Carry Yourself As Such

R.J. Jenkins

authorHOUSE®

AuthorHouse™
1663 Liberty Drive
Bloomington, IN 47403
www.authorhouse.com
Phone: 833-262-8899

Published by AuthorHouse 02/03/2021

ISBN: 978-1-6655-1533-7 (sc)
ISBN: 978-1-6655-1534-4 (e)

Library of Congress Control Number: 2021901665

Print information available on the last page.

This book is printed on acid-free paper.

Contents

1

a man by nature
is a provider

Fellaz this does not mean only financially providing it means making a way to provide whatever your child or significant other may need. But it is not specific to kids & spouses it goes for anyone you care about. friend family neighbor coworker or the old lady carrying her own groceries at the market. you provide whatever it takes to uphold your community. the sad reality is most of us grow up being taught to only provide for our kids. oh and provide for mama but only if you get rich, but stop n think for a second if all we all provide for is our offspring and maybe mama who providing for pops, sis, bro, auntie, unc, see when it boil down to it we got to get back to being the village that's raising these babies. it take men to make men no matter what society tell you so as men we gotta PROVIDE these young boys with a blueprint to live by and not just the real nigga standard. who is protecting these young boys from the streets, who is protecting these young girls from being preyed upon, who is protecting our queens from abusive sexist derogatory treatment, who is protecting our kings from racial injustices, police brutality, social and corporate discrimination? If not us as men than who. the ladies or the babies cant be the warriors, and the older generation put their bid in so its up to us fellas.

2

a man by nature is a protector

this means exactly what it sounds like as a man
you protect all those who need protecting.
from the ant to the elephant at some point
in life every being needs protecting and as
men we take an unspoken oath to be that
source of protection by any and all means.
most importantly as men we gotta get back
to protecting each other. the fact that its
excepted in society to kill someone that
looks like you but you cant publicly gay bash
should tell you something. I mean you can
share a video of a black man being murdered in
cold blood and it will go viral but if you share
a video of you expressing disagreement with
the homosexual lifestyle in any way you or
your post will be blocked. so with that in mind

we gotta get on one accord and protect each other like we all are blood related. oh and for the record I mean protect each other's mental, physical, emotional, and spiritual well being. I believe this new generation has everything it takes to shift the culture except proper guidance and PROTECTION from the mostly self proclaimed OG's out here. we seen all our parents and grandparents be disrespected or worse simply because we have developed a it aint happen to me mentality and its literally a poison to our community. more so than any drug, alcohol, or diseases

3

a man by nature is a guider

it is your responsibility as a man to guide all those who fall under the sound of your voice to the highest form of themselves. teach the young dope boy to start his own business, teach that stripper how to invest her money into herself. teach that crackhead its life beyond a rock. teach that prostitute the true value of her body. most of us lack guidance and pretty much figure this shit out as we go along. it be generation after generation of trial and error, wrapped in mistakes and bad decisions, covered in failure and poverty. most of us got the game from people who aint have the game or aint been winning at it our whole lives. so we gotta step up and guide the next

generation into power and prosperity instead
of pain and poverty. imagine being responsible
for the uplifting of your entire bloodline
all it takes is focus and determination, but
more importantly the will to make it happen
regardless. I know, I know your family
wont listen and their all doing their own
thing. I learned that people only respond to
results not words no matter the substance.
don't take it personal just show and prove
and the right ones will follow suit when
the time is right, until then stay the course
king the end result will be well worth it.

4

a man by nature
is a problem solver

as men logic and understanding are the 2
most important tools you will ever possess. a
man should think, process, and strategically
move through any and every situation. Think
before you speak, think before you act but
most importantly think before you think. (I
wont explain but don't miss that 1) every
move whether reactive or proactive should
be strategically made with the goal of coming
to a conclusion with little to no casualties.
Don't let nobody tell you 2+2=4 because
3+1 might work better for you. what I'm
saying is find your own path but as long
as you reach the goal aint no wrong route.
it doesn't matter if you build the roof first
or the foundation as long as you fulfill the
process and get to the finished product.

still don't get it? the same way you can fly across country you can walk, it will for sure take much longer but if you don't quit sure enough you will eventually cover the ground you set out to cover. its nothing wrong with thinking your way through every situation, the smart man will always conquer the strong man in the end. why is that you ask? simply because the strong man will resort to power and force while the smart man will resort to logic and strategy. any fool can play checkers it don't take no intellect to full blast or set a mofo up. but chess on the other hand you must OUT THINK your opponent no matter the depth of their knowledge. that's why they say life is chess not checkers because you cant muscle your way through this game of life it requires finesse and strategy.

5

a man by nature is a logical thinker

THINK critically analyze every aspect, every angle, every outcome, every negative, every positive, every potential casualty, every potential gain, and every potential outlet. then its safe to make your decision. I know it sounds over the top but I promise its full proof, if you can remain level headed and always thinking aint too much you cant overcome. Fear and anger will always compromise your better judgement, but if you can process the situation for all outcomes I guarantee you will come up with a solution. best way to do this is by controlling your breathing for starters, the deeper the situations the deeper your breaths should be.

never forget PANICKING WILL COST YOU YOUR LIFE!!!! panicking is also due to the lack of processing a logical solution at the height of the moment. but what most don't know is your mind is already equipped for such scenarios so when you don't think critically you forfeit the power of the strongest muscle in your body. YOUR BRAIN!!!!!!! they say the mind is a terrible thing to waste, I say the power of the mind is a terrible thing to be unaware of.

6

a man by nature
is a king

as a man you are king of all you survey. every living breathing thing sits beneath your throne. BUT 2 things come with that, number 1 is just because you are king doesn't take away from the crown of any other man. you all are kings don't let social hierarchy and power structures make you believe kings cant or don't coexist. number 2 is you cant be a king but disrespect or harm other kings and queens. yes you are king, and of the highest magnitude might I add. but you also have a unspoken obligation to shine the crown of fellow kings and uphold the dignity of all kingdoms. I know you wondering how you maintain your status as king while fully acknowledging the crown of the next man. simple, Mercedes makes thousands of the exact same car but number 50,000 still doesn't devalue number 1 by even a cent. so yes you can be a king standing in a room full of kings in the same kingdom, and without a power struggle as well. oh and let me be real clear the size of your crown IS NOT determined in no way shape form or fashion by the size of or the lack of your castle. a homeless man is no less a king than the dude living in the gated community, and deserves the same level of dignity and respect. I'm a firm believer in the phrase "Kings Raise Kings" fellaz we gotta get back to molding the next generation of kings to be mightier than us. what good has allowing these boys to set their own standard for what it means to be a man done us?

7

a man by nature
is a way maker

when broken down to its simplest form this simply means (quote me on this) MAKE THAT SHIT HAPPEN KING!!! you have everything it takes to manifest all of your wildest dreams so as a man you just gotta make a way even when the path in front of you seems impossible. if you ask me the only things that cant be done are the things you don't try. if you try and it don't work try something different eventually you will at minimum accidently figure it out. say for instance you trying to assemble a piece of furniture but you don't have the instructions, I bet my last on the fact that if you keep trying it wont take half as long or half the effort as you thought it would. challenge your mind and your abilities you will surprise yourself at the things you can accomplish. no one ever said that the fastest or easiest path was the best one nor did anyone say it would yield the best results. yeah if you had the directions you would have put it together faster but trial and error teaches you not only how to do it but it sharpens your problem solving skills. not to mention the next time you wont need directions you will figure it out on confidence alone mark my words. I don't care if its the pot of gold at the end of the rainbow or the light at the end of the tunnel which ever floats your boat GET THERE! no matter if you scoot, crawl, walk, skip, jog, run, drive, sail, fly, or fuckin teleport set your destination and get there no matter the odds. the object of the game aint to win its to master the game winning is a reward that comes with it. we always taught to win but if we don't lose we don't evolve our game hints the saying if you want to be the best you got to beat the best. I say if you wanna be the best you gotta study the best and build on what you learn, why conquer the best when you could be the reason the best get better. beating mj on the court wouldn't have made nobody the best but the player who studies mj and masters his game will then be able to enhance what was learned can truly be the greatest player to ever grace the court.

8

a man by nature
is confidence
builder

I know the world make you cold hearted as
a man but you must be mindful of the words
that roll off your tongue. no matter who you
converse with let your words be empowering,
let them be uplifting, let them be a source of
strength for the weak, a boost of energy for the
tired, a source of joy to the disheartened. you
never know the power of one sentence until that
one sentence you utter saves or changes a life.
speak life into every one who you interact with
on any scale at any level of life. my mother told
me when I was locked up that I didn't have to
let it consume me I could be a light in that dark
place. I'm not going to say I actually listened
at the time but those words laid heavy on my
conscience. you know how much a kind word
mean to a hopeless person? or a compliment
to someone with low self esteem? how about a
word of encouragement to a suicidal person?

these are the small things that as men we fail to deliver to even the ones we love so imagine doing it for every person you encounter. we got to rebuild our village starting with the men. nothing wrong with a man checking another man because iron sharpens iron, but society has conditioned us to receive criticism as a form of disrespect. this did nothing but breed generation after generation of lost males finding their own path to nowhere. if we speak life into all of our brothers we can reconstruct our whole culture. which will in turn breed generations of literal super men standing on morals principles honor and respect and values set forth by refined re-educated and reborn MEN! and all this can be obtained by simply building the confidence of all men you encounter young and old. if you shine his crown he will be proud to show it to the world, so build up your brethren and watch as the paradigm shifts for the better.

9

a man by nature
is a consoler

every one in every walk of life will at
some point experience some level of pain,
undoubtedly. but as men we are conditioned
through life experiences to process and handle
pain better in most cases. I believe this to be
because in times of sorrow as men we need to
still be critical thinkers and hold down the fort
in dark times. not saying don't hurt or feel your
hurt or even express ya hurt simply saying you
are meant to be a shoulder to lean on cry on
and for them babies to ride on. so deal with it
as you may but be the cushion your children,
spouse, friends, neighbors, and even strangers
may need. I know you probably like what I look
like consoling a stranger but as I said before you
be surprised how much wiping a tear and saving
a life are equivalent. we got to get to the point
where we lead with love, if so the world will
be over saturated with love and compassion,

imagine your babies and grand babies growing up in a world filled with love and compassion. I know, its hard to imagine but it is very possible to manifest if we can all get on one accord at least the fellaz anyway. if us as men get on the same page then just as nature designed the women and lil ones will follow close behind. if nursing a young boys mental scars could rewrite the future lets start teaching our boys how to decipher, process, and finally deal with their feelings. lets show our girls they can go back to trusting men to protect them and provide for them not just financially. we be forgetting the broken homes and broken hearts we create when we take certain actions and make certain decisions on the street side of the fence. its our duty to rebuild both at any and all costs.

10

a man by nature is a soldier

always thinking, always prepared, always strategizing, always observing, always analyzing, always computing, always calculating, always navigating, always pre thinking, always militant, always disciplined, always ready for battle. if you stay ready you will stay ready!!! they say life is chess because EVERY single move you make can cost you more than you could ever regain. I heard once that a man isn't a man until he finds something he is willing to die for, truest shit if you ask me because if you are the only person you would die for you will be the only person you live for. wake up everyday with the mindset that you are at war, because in reality YOU ARE. you are at war with jealousy, greed, lust, hatred, miseducation, racial tension, poverty, intentional disease and ailments, mass incarceration, feminization, hyper sexualization, lack of resources, gmo's. the list goes on for days, so how could you not wake up battle ready each day you are able to part your eyelids. A key strategy in battle is knowing your opponent, in the streets we call it doing your homework on a nigga. knowing what you are up against can make all the difference in any situation simply because you retain control of the outcome. for example they say fight fire with fire, now granted this will make one hell of a bout. But I say fight fire with water, this will end the fight long before u feel the heat of your opponents fire. Remember your greatest victories are the ones you don't sustain any casualties obtaining. preparation minimizes casualties more than any attack strategy or defensive techniques by volumes. we all have come up short due to lack of preparation before but it is not a permanent circumstance grow, evolve, prepare, and kill shit.

II

a man by nature is a conqueror

anything or anyone that stands in the way of your finish line whatever that may be, FIRE AT WILL. not literally (in all cases) but figuratively destroy all obstacles and road blocks. think around it but bust through it like a full blown tornado, let your will power be a wrecking ball to anything hindering your path to your destiny. you gotta know within yourself that everything starts within yourself. anything you can think you can have, which is why the old folks stressed JUST PUT YOUR MIND TO IT! line em up & knock em down, be it goals, tasks, stats, problems, bills, burdens, grades, struggles, or anything for that matter. every man is born with 3 versions of himself in my opinion, the civilian you, the king you, and the godly you. it is completely up to you which version you choose to be, but don't get it confused you can definitely tap in to all 3. I came up with a acronym to help you fight this war and that is that you can (M)anifest (A)ll (N)eeds. going into battle knowing you can manifest your own victory signs the deal before you even hit the locker room. not saying you wont take losses. or endure some hurt & pain, or gain some scars but if you don't stop eventually winning is inevitable. the best fighters are the ones who don't fear losing. there is a huge difference between fighting to win and fighting not to lose. fighting to win means giving all you got in you from beginning to end, fighting not to lose means jus doing enough to not get beat and dragged.

if you take nothing else from this read let this settle in your mind your are director and leading actor of the hit movie titled "YOUR LIFE". meaning you are the director and starring actor in your life, everyone else is a extra in your movie. you have the ability to write your own story, and you can tackle any obstacle laid in front of you. I aint sayin I have the blueprint on perfection of the male species but EVERYTHING you just read applies to you as a man no matter who you are. so do yourself and you offspring's a favor and CARRY YOURSELF AS SUCH!!!!!!!!!!!! (from the womb to the grave)

Printed in the United States
By Bookmasters